Heywood

IN OLD PHOTOGRAPHS

Heywood

IN OLD PHOTOGRAPHS

JOHN HUDSON

Budding
BOOKS

A Budding Book

This book was first published in 1994 by
Sutton Publishing Limited
Phoenix Mill · Thrupp · Stroud
Gloucestershire · GL5 2BU

This edition first published in 2001 by
Budding Books, an imprint of
Sutton Publishing Limited

Copyright text © John Hudson, 1994

British Library Cataloguing in Publication Data.
A catalogue record for this book is available from
the British Library.

ISBN 1 84015 217 6

Typeset in 9/10 Sabon.
Typesetting and origination by
Sutton Publishing Limited.
Printed in Great Britain by
J.H. Haynes & Co. Ltd, Sparkford.

Contents

Municipal pride: a well-tended lake at Queen's Park.

Introduction

Heywood was in at the dawn of the Industrial Revolution, with the Makin Mill in operation by 1780 and evidence of bales of cotton being bought into town three years before that. Yet for all its textile trade pedigree, reminders of which still abound in some of the finest surviving mill buildings in Lancashire, it was always a place from which workers could escape in their precious leisure hours.

There were few truly urban people in the northern cotton trade, outside such hellish inner-city slums as Ancoats in Manchester. Even the mill girls and doffers of Heywood's big neighbours, Rochdale and Bury, knew what it was like to wander the moorlands on Sundays and warm summer evenings, and for the people of Heywood the opportunities were all the greater – not only the moors, but wooded valleys and dells, pretty by any standards, and the endless criss-cross of cinder tracks through green farmland over towards Birch and Simister. The influence of wealthy families, from the long-ago Heywoods to the Healeys of this century, has also left legacies to broaden the mind and lift the spirits. All in all, though there have been times when life in the town has been very tough indeed, there have always been the compensations of easy if fleeting escape.

Our forebears also had the blessing of companionship close at hand from tight-knit families, friends and workmates. Heywood, more than most, is a town of small centres of population stemming from scattered hamlets, and these gave its people focal points to their lives. So did churches and chapels of every denomination, clubs, pubs, football and cricket teams, debating societies, bands, choirs, carnival committees, mill social clubs and the hundred-and-one other means by which the Victorian town, in a phrase that's often derided today, made its own fun.

Church life was particularly strong; Heywood is scarcely a city of dreaming spires, but the Anglicans and Methodists in particular ensured that their flocks would not have far to walk on Sunday mornings. Then there were the little gas-lit cinemas, the flea-pits, the bug-huts, places loved and affectionately scorned in equal measure. The Gem, where the British Legion now stands; the Picturedrome in Market Street, where you'll now find Boots the Chemists; the Empire, on the site of the Civic Hall; the Palace, somewhere close to the aisles of Morrison's supermarket.

So what are we told by a selection of photographs such as this? We look at some of them and see filth, dilapidated property and evidence of life restricted by geographical and social boundaries, but it is at our peril that we confuse these limitations on our forebears' lifestyle with hardship as they would have understood the word. When life's as tough for your neighbour as it is for you, then that has no small influence on the way you look at the world. Besides, for all their scurrying around in a haze of Lowryesque coal smoke, it was often the case that Lancashire's cotton workers were by no means poor by the standards of their country cousins. If you were in work – if you and your wife and four of your children were in the mills, down to the half-time girls of twelve – you were a very inefficient manager indeed if poverty was a problem to you. As for comparisons of relative happiness – 'we were poor but we were happy' – let us set such thoughts aside. It is up to each of us to find ease and peace of mind where we can, and if we are less capable of doing it now than we were in previous generations, that is more a reflection on us as people than on the changing times. Certainly, by almost every objective judgement it is possible to apply, the quality of life within our grasp today is almost ridiculously superior to what we had to endure in the past.

The Victorian advertisements reproduced in this book are a reminder of the vast diversity of goods once produced in the town – porter, paper bags and much else in between. Some products were meant to go no farther than the local beerhouse, others to spread the name of Heywood throughout the world – but all of them gave the town a sense of purpose and destiny that was perhaps taken rather too much for granted until we woke up one morning and found they were gone. One enduring trait in the town is an interest in its roots and its heritage – and not surprisingly so, since what happened to Heywood and the other mill towns in the Industrial Revolution really was extraordinary. Today, and presumably for the rest of time, life in small-town Lancashire goes on and will go on much as it does in small-town Leicestershire or Derbyshire – the bypass, the discount warehouses, the sports centre, the video shops. But for 150 years Heywood and its peers were complete one-offs in the eyes of the rest of the world, the workshop of the universe, and it is a tradition to be prized.

'We made our own fun . . .'. Members of Boots the Chemists' drama group in 1955, one of scores of local societies covering a vast range of interests.

In my choice of photographs for this book I have tried to concentrate on human interest, and hope that I have not upset would-be contributors in doing so. What I have endeavoured to do is avoid good 1934 pictures that look like bad 1994 ones. It matters little to me if the shot shows the church tower before the ivy was cut away, or the mill before the 1926 extension was built. Give me the bewhiskered bowling club, the Whit Walks toddlers, the grimy apprentice lads. . . .

I hope all who have helped me are acknowledged on page 128, but I trust I shall offend nobody if I single out John Slawson of Hopwood for special mention. He is well known throughout town for his writings on local history, in books of his own and in the *Heywood Advertiser*, but nothing from my long experience of local historians led me to anticipate whole-hearted, sharply perceptive, resourceful and always cheerful cooperation of the kind I received from him. Several times in my travels around town I mentioned that John Slawson was helping me. And if, as was often the case, the reply was: 'Yes, of course, he's the local historian,' I would make it quite clear that there was no 'yes, of course' about it. The level of support he was giving me was far beyond the realm of 'yes, of course'. I fear this marked me as a crusty old stick in the eyes of some, and though it's an accusation to which I seem to be growing increasingly prone, I hope my true feelings for the town shine through in these pages.

John Hudson, 1994

SECTION ONE
Around the Town

It's possible that readers might know this scene. Producers of postcards clearly loved the view from Market Street up through Market Place to St Luke's Church, and it remains Heywood's best-known image to this day. What a difference the towering St Luke's must have made to the way the town looked to travellers passing through after its consecration in 1862, its spire visible for miles. Indeed local people, and not only Anglicans, felt equally impressed by this flamboyant landmark, and it is hard to believe that the later civic buildings in and around Hind Hill Street would have been built to such high specifications if it had not been for the inspiration of the church across the way. To the left of this picture, taken in around 1920, we see the large white sunblind of the Golden Boot and beyond it the Queen Anne Hotel – before it was black-and-white Tudor. In fact it dates from the 17th century, and once served wayfarers as a coaching inn and the local community as a petty sessional court and post office.

Fancy dress cycle parades were a great feature of life in Lancashire in Edwardian times, though it must be said that the men pushing their bikes at the front of this procession are in everyday attire. A fine example of our forebears' sense of occasion, this annual parade of the town band, local worthies, the fire engine and the rushcart brought everyone on to the streets – and on to the balcony of the Reform Club in the centre of the picture. Rush-bearing, around which the wakes holidays of towns in and around Rochdale and Oldham grew up, stemmed from the old tradition of laying new rushes on the floors of churches before winter set in. This worthy objective developed into a boozy fiasco in the early 19th century, but Victorian morality had tamed the festivities almost to the point of extinction by the turn of the century.

The Market Place and St Luke's Church in the early 1920s, with the newly introduced Tudor timbering of the Queen Anne building on the left.

The peal of bells at St Luke's was rehung in 1971, although the tenor was the only one taken away for repair. Here we see the scene, with, it must be said, not too many townsfolk waiting around to see whether the crane driver would drop a clanger.

Another well-known Heywood scene, looking down Bury Street towards Mellor's notorious leaning chimney. Not far away, the mill village of Rhodes was famous for having the tallest chimney in the Northern Union and far beyond. Heywood could not compete with that – but with one leaning four feet askew, it had the only shaft that had bypassers hoping the wind wouldn't blow too hard. They said New York Mill, to the left, had more spindles than any other in the world.

Farther down Bury Street towards Bridge Street, this is an interesting picture. Another postcard from the same Bell series, taken from within inches of the same point in the very early years of this century, shows Joseph Ogden's bootmakers in very old premises on the corner facing on to Peel Street. Here, perhaps ten years on, Nunwick's shop has taken its place in a new block facing the main road.

Scaffolding encases the top of St Luke's tower in this view up a quiet York Street from the front of the Ship Hotel in around 1920.

R. SHARROCKS,

10, MARKET PLACE, HEYWOOD,

CABINET MAKER AND UPHOLSTERER.

FURNITURE to suit all classes, made to order, suitable for either Mansion or Cottage.

SHOP and OFFICE FIXTURES and FURNITURE, and every Article in the Trade supplied, of first-rate quality and at reasonable prices.

JOHN LUCAS,

SADDLER,

AND HARNESS MAKER,

19, YORK STREET, HEYWOOD.

Every requirement for the horse and stable promptly and economically supplied. Manufacturer and repairer of Mackintosh and Oil Cloth Cart and Waggon Covers. Strapping for Machinery made and repaired.

J. C. OLDHAM,

MANUFACTURER OF ALL KINDS OF

SHUTTLES,

Dawson St., Heywood.

EXPORT AND OTHER ORDERS PROMPTLY EXECUTED.

To Cabinet Makers, Upholsterers, &c.

THOMAS TWEEDALE,

WOOLLEN FLOCK MANUFACTURER,

PILSWORTH ROAD, HEYWOOD.

OLD FLOCKS RE-WILLOWED.   ORDERS PROMPTLY EXECUTED.

Saddles, shuttles and stuffing for sofas. Heywood turned its hand to so many industries in Victorian times – and phrases such as 'old flocks re-willowed' remind us of the skills we have lost on our march towards mechanization.

Bury Old Road, *c*. 1910 – and all the time in the world for the errand boy to oblige the photographer by giving the picture a focal point.

Middleton Road, Hopwood, a scene still recognizable today, give or take a few thousand paving setts. On the right Jonty Ogden stands at the door of his Black Swan pub.

Canal Street, Hopwood, with terraces with distinctive arched doorways and lower windows.

The junction of Middleton and Manchester Roads at Hopwood, with St John's Church to the left. Older residents still know this spot as the Big Lamp, after a long-lost landmark that once stood here. Victorian or Edwardian engineers presumably felt the need to illuminate some awkward corners from a height somewhat above the norm – but it never failed to impress the locals, who invariably named the whole area after these phenomenal lamp-posts. Within a few miles of Heywood, both Shaw and Radcliffe were equally proud of their Big Lamps.

It was an event not to be sneezed at when the likeness-tekkin' man came to your street. You lined up to be photographed, and woe betide your mam if she wouldn't fork out the couple of coppers for your picture when the cameraman came around with his wares a few days later. One of the little boys in this group in Marlborough Street, Hopwood, is holding a well-worn cricket bat – and a little girl wears a mill worker's shawl, although she seems far too young to be a twelve-year-old half-timer.

Heywood station in Edwardian times, a facility that came into its own when the line from Castleton Blue Pits was extended to Bury in 1848; for the first seven years, from 1841, passengers had to put up with a horse-drawn service from Castleton – which, since 1970, is more of a service than they have now.

One of the seven electric trams in which Heywood Corporation bought a financial stake at their introduction in 1905. Before that, the town had been served by steam trams to Bury and Rochdale.

Rochdale Road East at Captain Fold some years before the First World War, and another of those quiet suburban scenes in which nothing happens but from which we can glean so much about small town life in the early years of the century.

SECTION TWO
Meet the Folks

You're not in HEYWOOD now So don't start Throwing your Weight about

Apart from being Monkey Towners, living on the other side of Bury from 'Ape' Bridge, old-time Heywood folk prided themselves on their refusal to be put upon. No doubt they enjoyed the spirit of this card – but in truth, nobody likes to be put upon, wherever they live, and its publisher, Charles Wilkinson of Manchester, presumably did very nicely by deleting Heywood in favour of Bury, Rochdale, Oldham and so ad infinitum. . . .

Irish-born Pat Loughlin arrived in Heywood in the 1880s and was 104 when he died in 1965. A keen football fan, on his hundredth birthday he was visited by the Manchester United management team of Matt Busby and Jack Crompton (see page 122).

Backroom boys at St Joseph's production of *Cinderella* in December 1949. Back, left to right: Arthur Hall, John Slawson, Tommy Carr, Tom Dunn and Danny Kelly; front, Jimmy Cunliffe and Tom Ingham. Below, from much the same period, the team for *Jack and the Beanstalk*.

The Hollywood choreography genius Busby Berkeley tried to beat the recession blues with his film *Gold Diggers of 1933*. But how could Dick Powell and Ruby Keeler compete with the charms of *Captain Fold Follies of 1933*?

Almost all of their menfolk still absent, the women and children of Marlborough Street smile for the camera on VJ Day, 15 August 1945.

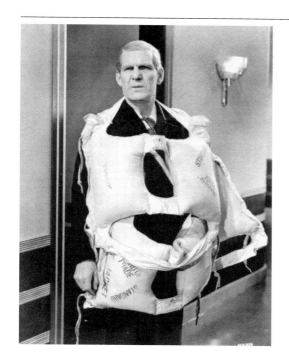

Will Hay as Heywood never knew him. The comic actor who flourished playing schoolmasters and petty officials, seen here in a romp called *Hey, Hey, USA*, was an apprentice at Smith's Sun Iron Foundry.

Just as everyone in Swansea had a drink with Dylan Thomas, everyone in Heywood remembers something that happened to Julie Goodyear, a local publican's daughter, when she were a lass. Not that she's strayed too far; Coronation Street's Bet Lynch still has a house in town.

And then there's the small matter of Lisa Stansfield, superstar. It seemed that for years her friends and relatives were telling the local press that she had a voice that would take the world by storm, but it's not always easy to cast the girl from the local comprehensive school in the role of a globe-trotting chart-topper. The picture on the left was taken not long after she made the number one spot in October 1989 with her second hit record, 'All Around the World'.

Not a corner of Heywood you will recognize. In fact it's the town's eighteen-year-old Lance Corporal Harold Partington in Egypt with his pals in October 1914. The next time he hit the local headlines, in the following May, was in the most tragic circumstances – as one of the first seven casualties of the Lancashire Fusiliers' disastrous Gallipoli campaign.

Heywood Home Guard on parade in Church Street behind their commanding officer Mr Wilson, looking considerably younger and fitter than their *Dads' Army* counterparts.

The Heywood English Concertina Prize Band in Edwardian times, with their bandmaster S. Jackson and two brave young women flanking him. Lancashire towns prided themselves on their catholic musical tastes – Wigan had a thriving mandolin college – but can you imagine the kind of noise made by thirty strong men and true playing concertinas?

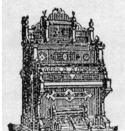
More manifestations of musicality in Heywood, this time in Victorian times, when the word 'professor' was used rather more loosely than it is today.

St John's Scout officials at around the time of the troop's move from Rock Street to a new headquarters beside Hopwood Recreation Ground in September 1972.

Far from alone among small towns, Heywood was unhappy to lose its borough council status when it was merged into the Rochdale Metropolitan Borough in 1974. Seen here is the last Borough Mayor, the late Councillor Leonard Nuttall, with his wife and Mayoress Mrs Vera Nuttall.

The Elite Concert Company of Heywood. The message on the back of the postcard says: 'Dear Vincent, if you can bring a few eggs please do so.' Surely not to pelt the Elite?

In the spirit of the mythical bird, the Phoenix ringers have revived the handbell tradition at St Luke's. Here they are seen at a festival of carols in December 1991.

It was Sunday best for St Luke's bellringers and their friends in 1911 when they travelled to the Gillett and Johnston foundry in Croydon to see their peal being recast.

St Luke's bellringers in the mid-1950s. Back, left to right: Henry Welbourne, Rene Kilpatrick, Alan Crabtree, John Partington, Ernest Brearley and Geoffrey Mills; front: Peter Butterworth, Keith Jarvis, Tom Hurst, Philip Turner and Roger Maher.

Manchester Road Methodists boasted some fine singers in the mid-1950s, and they used their talents to full effect in the revue *Paris in Spring*.

Happy when they're hiking: staff of Edward Taylor's tailor's shop on a day out to the Ingleton area, 1930s.

SECTION THREE

Church Life

New Jerusalem Church in Edwardian times.

The fun of dressing up: women from St Luke's Church outside the vicarage during the course of some olde-tyme antics. One of them is dressed as a man, complete with luxuriant moustache.

A more conventionally dressed group at St Luke's vicarage at around the time of the First World War.

A group from St Joseph's at Wavertree, visiting a member of the congregation who had become a nun.

Church and other bazaars were big business in late Victorian and Edwardian days. They could raise £2,000 at a time when £100 a year was a living wage, and some of them would go on for several days, with a different opener each afternoon. There would always be a brochure to go with these events, fat with advertising and with long lists of names of willing helpers to run the stalls. They were controversial. Many clergymen and more spiritual members of their flock didn't like them – but if there was a roof to be repaired or a Sunday school to be built, there was no denying their pulling power. This unidentified bazaar, before the crowds rolled in, was pictured by the Heywood photographer C.E. Willis. The stall on the left is selling exclusively dolls, while the one on the right offers an intriguing array of linens, bric-a-brac, paintings and those good old standbys, decorated coat-hangers.

The lads of St Joseph's young men's club at the outbreak of the Second World War; Father Austin Ronan, on the right, joined up almost immediately, and is already in khaki. The other priests are Father Michael Murphy and Canon Richard Vereker.

The dilapidated chapel that was replaced by St Luke's Church in 1862. Although much altered, it was hopelessly inadequate to serve the burgeoning town, and was demolished after the Christmas Day service of 1859. The first chapel, an offshoot of the Bury parish, was built before 1552.

The extraordinary interior of the first St John's Church at Hopwood, one of those corrugated iron structures often known as tin churches. This picture from around 1900 shows it lavishly adorned with mock Gothic arches and biblical inscriptions, while the profusion of flowers suggests that it is perhaps harvest festival. By the turn of the century the congregation was determined to replace it with a more substantial structure, and late in 1902 they set out to raise £1,000 – through a bazaar.

Three of the key men responsible for raising funds to build the present St John's Church at Hopwood – left, the curate-in-charge, the Revd F.W. Cleworth, and below, churchwardens George Bell and Councillor R. Grundy.

The great day – laying the foundation stone for the new church at St John's, Hopwood, on 29 August 1903. As always in crowd pictures of this time, the women's hats impress – and as so often at turn-of-the-century stone-laying ceremonies, the contractors grasp their share of the glory by having their name writ large on the hoist.

Complementary pictures of a well-loved outlying place of worship, Ashworth Chapel, and its neighbouring Chapel House.

SECTION FOUR
Working Lives

The classic corner shop, Albert Birch's in Canal Street. Preston Alcock's Most Exquisite Tea is two shillings a pound, soda water is fivepence a flagon and Albert's array of enamel signs advertises everything from Hudson's, Sunlight, Watson's Matchless and Dr Lovelace's Soap to Fry's Chocolate and Cocoa.

When Edward Taylor ran his clothes shop in York Street it was a place for second-hand bargains. The boy standing in front of him in this picture, partly obscured by the little child in the big hat, is his son George – who in years to come, while retaining his father's name on the sign, turned it into a high-class tailoring and outfitting business that gave employment to many local people and did better than most in surviving the depression of the 1930s.

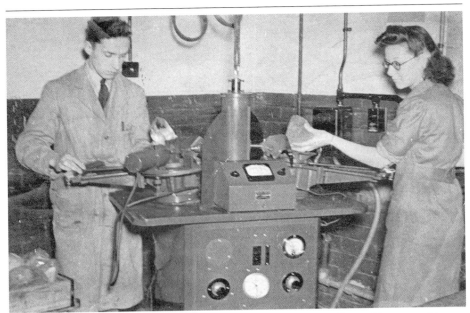

John Slawson and Violet Pinder testing crystal structures with an X-ray machine at Salford Electrical Instruments' Burns Mill, *c.* 1945.

The inspection room staff at Burns Mill celebrate the end of the war by stepping out on to the roof.

Salford Electrical Instruments alternated between Birch Mills and Burns Mill during the war. This is the test room at Birch Mills. The firm made crystal homing devices for bombers and fighters.

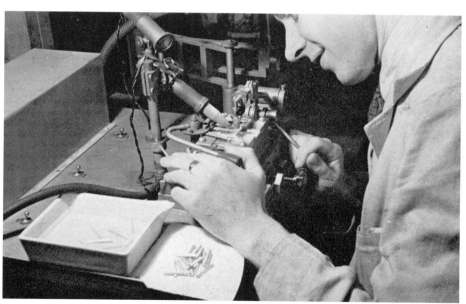

The quaintly named Tramping Cat drift mine in Simpson Clough in 1895, with coal being loaded on to a horse-drawn cart. Although largely beyond living memory, coal mining played a significant part in the local economy of much of the area around Bury in the 19th century.

Second World War production of jettison fuel tanks at Bridge Hall Mills, Heap Bridge.

This Preparation is highly recommended by **Medical Practitioners** as being the best form for the administration of Quinine, and as a **Tonic** and **Stomachic** far preferable to **Orange Quinine Wine, Bitter Beer,** &c.

Diluted with ten times its bulk of water, it forms a most wholesome and refreshing **Beverage.** It is particularly valuable in cases of **Indigestion, Loss of Appetite,** Neuralgic **Affections** and **Debility,** the result of **Fever,** overwork, or other causes. For **Consumption,** taken in conjunction with Cod Liver Oil, it is very beneficial.

The Manufacturer is continually receiving letters, testifying to the value of this Preparation. The following are selected out of many :—

From JAMES EDMUNDS, Esq., M. D., Lecturer on Medical Science to the London Female Sick Society.

"It is a nice preparation, free from any objection, and will accomplish every purpose of Quinine as a tonic. I hope it will come into general use in place of the Quinine Wine now so much used."

From ROBERT MARTIN, Esq., M.D., Physician to the Warrington Dispensary.

"I have now given your *Syrup of Orange and Quinine* a fair trial; it has not only answered admirably, but has been much liked in the cases in which I have prescribed it. I congratulate you on having presented to the profession so very elegant and useful a preparation.

From J. W. BEAUMONT, Esq., M.D., L.R.C.P., Edinburgh.

"I have subjected BECKETT'S *Syrup of Orange and Quinine* to a fair trial in cases such as are usually benefitted by Quinine, and have no hesitation in saying that it is *the best form and preparation of Quinine I have yet used.*"
Hanover Square, Sheffield.

From the "Chemist and Druggist."

"This elegant preparation, which has been introduced as a substitute for Orange Quinine Wine, is likely to become a popular remedy. We have had some personal experience of the effects of this preparation, and have no reason to doubt the statement of its inventor, that each fluid ounce contains two grains of Howard's Quinine."

From Mr. L. LORD, Registered Chemist, Rawtenstall.

"Sir,—Please to send, as soon as possible, six dozen pints and six dozen half-pints of your *Syrup of Orange and Quinine,* as our doctors are recommending it to all their convalescent patients. Some of my friends, who have been in the habit of drinking *Bitter Beer* to dinner, have adopted your *Syrup of Orange and Quinine* as a substitute, and declare it to be better both in cheapness and utility."

Ask for "Beckett's Syrup of Orange and Quinine,"

Prepared by W. BECKETT, Pharmaceutical Chemist, Heywood, Manchester,

AS QUININE WINE IS OFTEN SUBSTITUTED.

SOLD IN BOTTLES, Half-pints, 1s. 9d. ; Pints, 3s. **MAY BE PROCURED THROUGH ANY CHEMIST.**

If quinine was your poison, there was no finer way to take it in Victorian times than through Beckett's Syrup, Heywood-made and a health-encouraging three shillings a pint.

Heywood apprentices, possibly in the plastering trade, photographed by the local cameraman Tom Kirkman.

All aboard the chara for an outing from Isherwood's Mill, *c.* 1918.

T. W. HAZLEDEN & CO.,

Saddle, Collar,

AND

Harness Makers.

MARKET PLACE, HEYWOOD.

(OPPOSITE THE STAR INN.)

Dealers in Travelling Trunks and Portmanteaus.

Also Makers of CART and WAGON COVERS, and HORSE CLOTHING of the Best Quality—Prices on Application.

ALL ORDERS BY POST PROMPTLY ATTENDED TO.

In a world in which a significant minority of the population was four-legged, there was room for several saddle and harness makers in a town the size of Heywood.

The four Taylor sisters from the York Street tailoring family are among this group of workers at Dawson Hill Mill, now the site of Boots' warehouse. The work shed is festooned with paper chains as mills were on their rare high days and holidays, and the message seems to read Health And Happiness To The Bride And Bridegroom And Success To The Firm. An offspring of the boss getting married? It could be; but it doesn't look as if anyone – workers or the happy pair – is being encouraged to get carried away to the detriment of their work.

Order assemblers and their bosses, Boots' warehouse, mid-1950s.

Where's Our Gracie warbling 'Sing As We Go'? Workers leave the Mutual Mills, 1950.

A misty view of Green Lane Mill, 1950s.

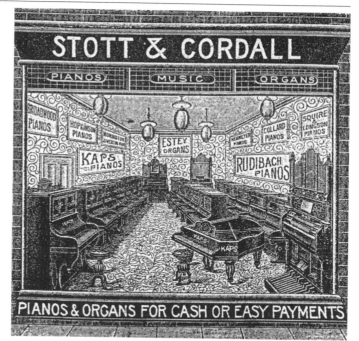

In 1902 Stott and Cordall's of Hornby Street were trying to sell pianos with the appealing line: 'As the opportunity of celebrating a Coronation has not before presented itself for nearly 70 years, you had better do something to keep this glorious event fresh in your memory. . .'.

1953, another Coronation – and the bunting flutters over Kenworthy and Holland's bread shop and grocery in Bamford Road.

It's still the Coronation year of 1953, this time at Partington's shop in York Street. At that address since 1895, but stemming from an even older-established business, it finally succumbed to the DIY giants in 1963. Below, Aaron Partington was one of the firm's Victorian forerunners, though his real speciality was as a slater.

AARON PARTINGTON,

No. 8, BAMFORD ROAD (NEAR THE MARKET PLACE), HEYWOOD,

SLATER,

PLASTERER AND PAINTER,

DEALER IN

North Country and Welsh Slates,

PLAIN & ORNAMENTAL RIDGE TILES.

CEMENTS, MASTIC AND PLASTER OF PARIS,

Chimney Tops, Sanitary Tubes, Fire Brick,

And all kinds of Fire Clay Goods, &c., &c.

Chimney Tops always on hand to cure Smoky Chimneys.

JAMES SCHOFIELD,

PLASTERING,

PAINTING, SLATING,

And General Repairs executed by Contract or otherwise.

Slates, Tiles, and a variety of Chimney Tops always in Stock.

68, MANCHESTER STREET,

HEYWOOD.

All enquiries immediately attended to.   J. S. solicits your patronage.

Mid-19th-century reminders that Aaron Partington had it by no means all his own way when he offered Heywood a painting and decorating service.

JAMES LIVSEY,

Painter, Paper-hanger,

GILDER, SIGN WRITER, &c.,

32, BRIDGE STREET,

HEYWOOD.

DECORATIONS

OF EVERY DESCRIPTION CONNECTED WITH THE TRADE.

PAPER HANGINGS of the latest Design constantly in Stock.

All Orders punctually attended to, personally superintended, and executed by Experienced Workmen.

Staff at St Joseph's School, 1930s. Back, left to right: Mr Doyle, Miss Law, Miss Biddie Dowling, Miss Roche, Miss Yates and John Mahon; front: Miss Geraghty, Hughie Doran, Father Smythe, William Arthur Maguire (headmaster) and Miss Bessie Calderwood. Mr Doyle married Miss Law, Miss Roche wrote children's stories, Mr Doran was a billiards ace and when Biddie Dowling caned you you stayed caned.

Great to be Young

Headmistress Mrs Hall with Queen Street School's children, 1903.

Queen Street School's youngsters three years later in 1906, headmaster Mr Tetlow on the right.

Good neighbours: Marlborough Street children line up for the travelling photographer in the early 1920s.

Harwood Park Infants, *c.* 1910.

Miss Calderwood's class at St Joseph's School, early 1930s.

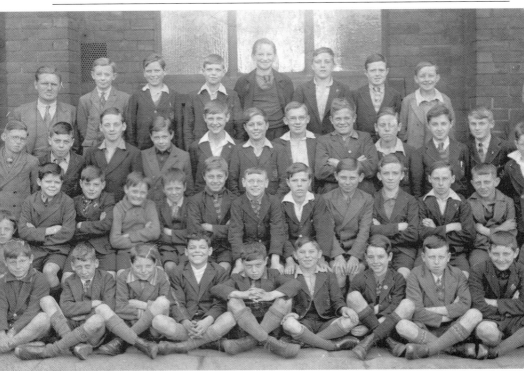

Boys at St Joseph's School in 1932 with their headmaster Mr Maguire on the left and class teacher Mr Doran on the right. The boy showing a good deal of white shirt towards the middle of the second row from the back is Gerard Heaney, who went on to make his name as the broadcaster Tom Heaney. The third boy from the right in the same row is John Slawson, the prominent local historian.

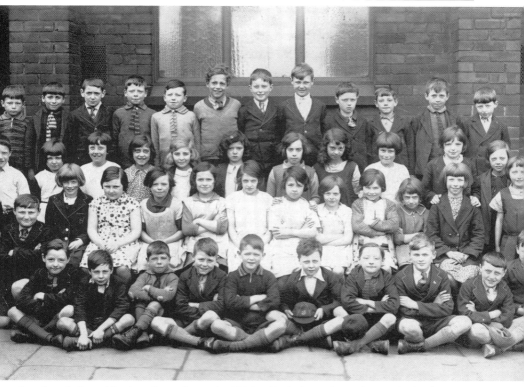

Another St Joseph's class from the early 1930s. Sixth from the right on the back row is Jack Cragg, who emigrated to become a leading surgeon in the United States.

Glad that's over. . . . Mona Heath, Emily Knight and Nora Thornton relax after the 1933 Whit Walk.

Sunny day, heavy stockings: Guides at Birtle, *c.* 1930.

Golden times: Heywood Guides at camp in the 1930s.

St John's Scouts on parade in very shiny boots on very muddy terrain at around the time of the First World War.

St John's Scout drummers at Rock Street School, their former HQ, *c.* 1960.

An early photograph of the 3rd St John's Scouts at camp in 1912.

The St John's boys at camp at Hesketh Bank, near Southport, in 1913. Doubtless the older ones would see a great deal more of camping in the following five years.

More vintage memories of the outdoor life with the St John's troop.

St John's Scouts in a field behind the Chapel House at Ashworth in around 1927. Not all the boys are identified, but it is generally agreed that the black dog atop the cart is called Peter.

St John's Cubs and Scouts at the opening of their new HQ at Hopwood Recreation Ground in 1972.

St John's Scouts on the march, 1972.

Guides on a Whit Walk, 1950s.

SECTION SIX
Heap Bridge

Heap Bridge early this century, a scene in which most of the property has been swept away. The factory chimney belonged to Yates Duxbury, who with Transparent Paper gave Heap Bridge a name for paper manufacture that was known throughout the world.

Heap Bridge, *c*. 1910, a Bury–Heywood tram on the right.

The other bridge for which Heap Bridge was known, the Seven Arches railway viaduct.

Another view of the bridge in around 1910 – some years before the increasingly
necessary road widening.

The year moves on to 1958, and a number 14 bus passes the Bury boundary sign on its way to Heywood. On the left, a sign points the circuitous way down to Transparent Paper, while straight ahead the Yates Duxbury chimney still dominates the scene.

The Bridge Inn, c. 1905, a popular landmark on the route between Heywood and Bury.

On the left, the Bridge Inn – and in the foreground of this picture from 1905, J. Smith's shack-like painter's and decorator's depot. Advertising signs for Cadbury's Chocolate and St Bruno suggest that it might have served as a shop at some earlier time.

TURNER & PARKER,

ALEXANDRA WORKS,

ROCHDALE ROAD, HEYWOOD.

MANUFACTURING CHEMISTS,

PAPER MERCHANTS,

AND

Paper Bag Manufacturers,

Soda Ash, Soda, Scouring Crystal, Soap Powder, Washing Powder, Dry Soap, Starch, Powder Blue.

WHEEL GREASE & BOILER COMPOSITION.

Victorian advertisements that serve as a reminder that Transparent Paper and Yates Duxbury were by no means alone in the paper manufacturing business in Heywood.

EDWIN HARDMAN,

THE NOTED

Paper Merchant & Paper Bag Manufacturer,

BRADSHAW ST., HEYWOOD.

EVERY DESCRIPTION OF PAPER BAGS KEPT IN STOCK. CASING BROWN'S CAP, BUTTER, AND TEA PAPERS, AND ALL KINDS OF GROCERY PAPERS.

Wholesale Houses supplied at the Lowest Possible Terms.

ALL ENQUIRIES BY POST PROMPTLY ATTENDED TO.

N.B.—Any Article not in stock procured without delay.

A bleak winter's scene looking south towards Gorsey Brow and Heap Bridge in 1936. The buildings in the picture at Higher Gorsey Brow Farm were demolished to make way for the M66, which has changed the Heap Bridge area around the bridge beyond all recognition.

The long and winding road at Heap Brow in 1965. The tower blocks of Darn Hill are by now part of the landscape, while the horizon centre and right is still dominated by the Air Ministry Maintenance Unit, at one time the town's major employer but by '65 just two years from closure.

Transparent Paper's main entrance at Bridge Hall Mills in around 1930. Paper making began on the site in 1716 and was stepped up considerably in the 19th century by the Wrigley family of Bury. Transparent Paper, another major Heywood employer, moved in in 1928, and the site is now in the hands of the international conglomerate Printpack Europe Ltd.

Victorian entrepreneurs who brought booming prosperity to Bridge Hall Mills: Thomas Wrigley, left, and his second son Oswald Osmond.

An odd mixture of the industrial and the romantic can be seen in many parts of Heywood and its fringes – perhaps most notably around Ashworth Valley, a glorious spot that nevertheless has seen industries as diverse as textiles and coal mining. This picture at Heap in the 1960s shows us Timberhurst farm buildings, formerly known as Woolner Hall.

Bridge Hall Mills in 1956, with the then new western section prominent. At a time when so much manufacturing capacity has been lost to Britain, this great plant still plays a major part in the economy of the area.

High Days and Whit Walks

What a splendid occasion, the visit of George V and Queen Mary on 12 July 1913. As could be imagined of a community that packed the streets for bicycle parades, the townsfolk were taking their places hours in advance to glimpse two faces they knew only from grainy black and white newspaper photographs or idealized souvenirs. The royal couple later moved on to Bury, and from Heap Bridge onwards they encountered more noisy and enthusiastic crowds.

On the day of the royal visit, this group connected with the Rose Day charity gathered together and posed for a picture in Queen's Park.

May Sunday, the Roman Catholics' walking day in Heywood, at St Joseph's in 1951.

Pretty prints and white gloves: St Luke's Anniversary Walk, *c.* 1960.

Some people always seemed more happy about walking than others: St Luke's Whit Walk, 1956.

1950s fashion to the fore as the women of the congregation walk on a St Joseph's May Sunday.

The rose queen and her attendants at the old St Luke's playground in Queen's Park Road, Whit Walk, 1958. Even then the tradition was so strong that it would have been hard to imagine that in just a few short years it would die away.

Britannia rules Bamford Road, St Luke's Whit Walk, 1930s.

The day was wet but this St John's Church parade, above and on the facing page, went ahead with all good cheer. Eton collars for the little boys, floral hats for the young women; there is much flamboyance in these pictures, in spite of their superficially sombre appearance. The byway off to the right is Rock Street.

Sunshine for St Joseph's May Sunday, *c*. 1950.

Some interesting expressions at the Anglican Whit Walk of 1952.

More groups from the Church of England walk of 1952.

Again it's 1952 – and what a fine view of the now demolished Star Hotel, on the corner of Bamford Road and Market Street, as the band marches smartly up towards St Luke's Church.

1952 – and wasn't it always the case that the band stopped playing just as it came up to pass you?

Hymn singing on the platform at the end of the walk.

The rose queen ceremony – who would have thought there could be such magic on the back of a lorry?

SECTION EIGHT

On the Fringes

Away from it all at Ashworth Valley.

Ashworth Bridge, a spot loved by generations of Heywood folk.

A third view of lovely Ashworth Valley, this time being contemplated by a young man dressed in his Sunday best.

Old property by tranquil water at Simpson Clough.

Hopwood memories: above, Hopwood Hall with its conservatory and sweeping grounds, and below, a more homely scene at Ogden Hall. Hopwood Hall is now part of a bustling college campus.

Carr Wood, where rushing waters flow – except if we have a dry spell.

Technically, Queen's Park really was presented to the people of Heywood by Queen Victoria. In reality some money from the estate of a rich townsman, Charles Martin Newhouse, devolved to the Duchy of Lancaster, and that's how it came about. The ceremony took place in 1879 and it left Heywood with a marvellous facility. It's not always easy to transform Victorian pleasure grounds into 1990s assets, however, especially with council budgets so tight; but a group of conservationists is taking a close interest in the park and the ways it can survive more or less intact. There is no municipal boating on the lake these days – but scores of anglers use it, not to mention a heron and a flock of Canada geese.

The classical Bamford Hall, standing sadly neglected in the middle 1950s, a decade more concerned with building the new than restoring the old. Its demolition was one of the most insensitive acts of the post-war years.

Another lost property, this time a row of old cottages at Doctor Fold Lane in Birch.

The M62 south of the town now runs over this stretch of the Heywood spur of the Rochdale Canal on which young Robert Slawson paddled his canoe in the early 1960s.

This Sporting Life

There's still a bowling green at Summit, but players now look little like the club members who trod its sward back in the 1890s.

St Joseph's, always a force to be reckoned with in the Heywood Sunday Schools League in the 1920s.

Heady Hill School footballers in 1928, known as the Cloggers. Because they were a dirty team? No, just look at the footwear of the boy on the right.

Heywood's Jack Livsey and his pal J. Littler at the far point of their 1,050-mile jaunt to John O'Groats in 1934.

Sporty type: Tom Oliver, shop assistant at Edward Taylor's tailor's shop, steps out in style in Blackpool, 1932.

It's always nice to win a trophy. Harwood Park youngsters and their teachers seem pleased about it in the 1958–9 season.

An international sporting night at Heywood Civic Hall in 1967, hosted by the then highly successful Bury Athletics Club. On the right is their 1964 Olympics competitor Mary Hodgson, while in the centre is the New Zealand runner Mollie Sampson.

Percy wasn't much of a name for an Isle of Man TT ace, so they called him Tim Hunt, and his exploits with the Norton team were read about with great interest in his native Heywood.

Casting off: Heywood Girl Guides prepare for a spot of strenuous rowing in the 1930s.

There was much excitement around Hopwood in 1961 when Pat Loughlin celebrated his hundredth birthday with the help of Manchester United's manager Matt Busby and trainer Jack Crompton.

Heywood Cricket Club in around 1920, towards the end of captain Dr H.H.I. Hitchon's playing days. Like W.G. Grace he was strictly an initials man, and nobody round the comfortable clubhouse at Crimble today can recall his Christian names – not even older club members who say with some pride that they were brought into the world by him. He was president from 1923 to 1929 and later a president of Lancashire. Heywood were founder members of the Central Lancashire League in 1892 and have been champions eleven times, the first in 1904 and most recently in 1984.

There was something worth getting dressed up for in 1929 when Heywood did the treble – the league championship, the knock-out Wood Cup and the aggregate trophy.

The Crimble cricket ground in 1921, the year Heywood moved there from Pot Hall. There is not a more attractive ground in the league, and the man to thank for acquiring it is David Healey, a member of one of the most influential families in the town's history. From the pavilion there are fine views over fields, woodlands and the park – and looking back into town the Mutual Mills dominate the skyline, an increasingly arresting sight as more and more of their kind are demolished.

There was another triple crown in 1945, marked by the presentation of the trophies to skipper Bill Farrimond by president James Hunt.

The treble winners of 1945. Standing directly behind captain Farrimond is Alan Wharton, who went on to play for Lancashire and England.

Some to watch: Heywood's under-18 team of 1988, Taylor and Whittaker Cup winners.

The knockout Wood Cup – the same trophy has been around since the early days – came Heywood's way again in 1993, to the delight of captain David Fare.

Acknowledgements

Thanks for the loan of pictures, background information and other help are due to:

David Appleton • Brian Beal • Revd John Brocklehurst • Bury Metro Libraries
John Carter • Lilias Coleman • Vera Duerdin • Peter Garvey
The *Heywood Advertiser* • Biwater Heywood Cricket Club
Heywood Pensioners' Group • Sheila Hill • Val Hopkinson • Phyllis Hudson
Revd and Mrs Clifford Knowles • E. Leigh • Joan Lord • Peter Morgan
John Partington • Printpack Europe Ltd • Edgar Richardson
St John's Church • John Slawson • Bill Watson